MILITARY ENGINEERING
★ ★ ★ ★
IN ACTION

MILITARY HUMVEES

ARMORED MOBILITY

Taylor Baldwin Kiland and Michael Teitelbaum

E **Enslow Publishing**
101 W. 23rd Street
Suite 240
New York, NY 10011
USA
enslow.com

Published in 2016 by Enslow Publishing, LLC.

101 W. 23rd Street, Suite 240, New York, NY 10011

Library of Congress Cataloging-in-Publication Data

Kiland, Taylor Baldwin, 1966–
    Military Humvees : armored mobility / Taylor Baldwin Kiland and Michael Teitelbaum.
        pages cm. — (Military engineering in action)
    Includes bibliographical references and index.
    Summary: "Describes the development, use, and abilities of Humvees in the military"—Provided by publisher.
    Audience: Grades 7-8.
    ISBN 978-0-7660-6914-5 (library binding)
    ISBN 978-0-7660-7065-3 (pbk.)
    ISBN 978-0-7660-7066-0 (6-pack)
    1. Hummer trucks—United States—Juvenile literature. 2. Iraq War, 2003-2011—Juvenile literature I. Teitelbaum, Michael.
II. Title.
    UG618.K55 2015
    355.8'3—dc23

                    2015011220

Printed in the United States of America

To Our Readers: We have done our best to make sure all Web site addresses in this book were active and appropriate when we went to press. However, the author and the publisher have no control over and assume no liability for the material available on those Web sites or on any Web sites they may link to. Any comments or suggestions can be sent by e-mail to customerservice@enslow.com.

Portions of this book originally appeared in *Humvees: High Mobility in the Field*.

Photo Credits: © AP Images, p. 30; Benjamin Lowy/Getty Images, p. 13; Courtesy of ILNGPAO/US Army (soldiers in snow, front right), p. 1; Cpl. James L. Yarboro, US Marine Corps/Wikimedia Commons/Humvee in difficult terrain.jpg/public domain, p. 18; DoD photo by Lance Cpl. E.J. Young, US Marine Corps, p. 15; John Moore/Getty Images News/Getty Images, p. 44; JOHN MOTTERN/AFP/Getty Images, p. 45; Liu Jin/AFP/Getty Images, p. 4; Mike H/Shutterstock.com, p. 2; NICOLAS ASFOURI/AFP/Getty Images, p. 41; PATRICK BAZ/AFP/Getty Images, p. 21; PETRAS MALUKAS/AFP/Getty Images, p. 33; Philip Lange/Shutterstock.com, p. 47; Scott Peterson/Getty Images News/Getty Images, pp. 28, 40; Shutterstock.com (art/backgrounds throughout book): Dianka Pyzhova, Ensuper, foxie, kasha_malasha, pashabo; STAN HONDA/AFP/Getty Images, p. 42; US Air Force photo by Senior Master Sgt. David H. Lipp, p. 23; US Air Force photo by Staff Sgt. Heather Cozad, p. 35; US Air Force photo by Staff Sgt. Joshua T. Jasper, p. 34; US Army, p. 7; US Army photo by Sgt 1st Class Michel Sauret (humvee, front left), p. 1; US Army photo by Sgt. Joshua Laidacker, 4th IBCT, 3rd ID, Public Affairs, p. 36; US Army photo by Sgt. Ken Scar, 7th MPAD, p. 8; US Army photo by Sgt. Michael J. MacLeod, p. 25; US Army photo by Spc. Micah E. Clare, p. 17; US Army photo by Staff Sgt. Gina Vaile-Nelson, 133rd MPAD, Kentucky National Guard, p. 9; US Navy photo by Mass Communications Specialist 1st Class, Joshua Hammond, p. 39; US Navy photo by Mass Communications Specialist 2nd Class Bryan Weyers, p. 43; US Navy photo by Photographer's Mate 3rd Class Shawn Hussong, p. 29.

Cover Credits: Courtesy of ILNGPAO/US Army (soldiers in snow, front right); US Army photo by Sgt 1st Class Michel Sauret (humvee, front left); Shutterstock.com: kasha_malasha (camouflage background), foxie (series logo), Mike H (humvee, back).

CONTENTS

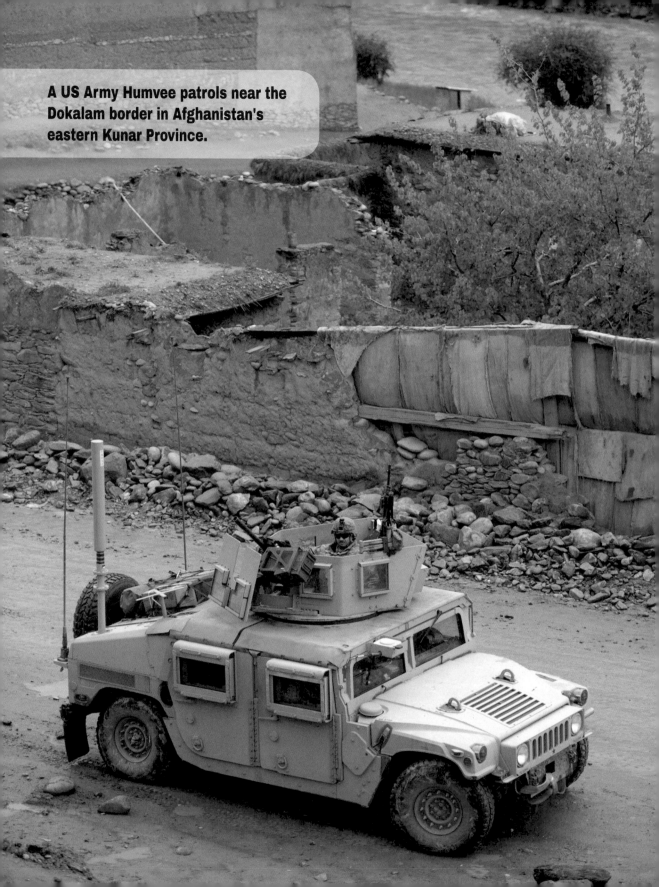

A US Army Humvee patrols near the Dokalam border in Afghanistan's eastern Kunar Province.

MRAPs: Saving Lives from IED Attacks

"We were driving down this unimproved road and that's when we ran over an improvised explosive device that was well buried and concealed under the road." Marine Corps Gunnery Sergeant Tim Colmer remembers the incident vividly. "When we ran it over, it blew up directly under the seat of the individual sitting behind me. It picked up our vehicle and moved us off the side of the road a good ten feet. It blew off the entire passenger side of the vehicle—all the way down to the armor. The tires were incinerated—they were gone. My sergeant who was in charge of security told me that when this device blew up, he couldn't see the vehicle. It was completely engulfed in flames, dust and debris. . . . All of us got out of the vehicle. We were all ambulatory, walking around the vehicle in pure amazement."

This vehicle, called a mine-resistant ambush-protected vehicle, or MRAP, was credited with saving the lives of Colmer and his crew. The MRAP has been used in Iraq and Afghanistan since 2007. Prior to that time, improvised explosive devices, or IEDs, were killing and severely injuring thousands of military service members. IEDs can be hidden in everyday objects like plastic bags, orange crates, or rusted gasoline cans. Soldiers driving vehicles cannot tell them apart from normal roadside garbage. Some IEDs have even been stuffed into the bodies of dead animals. IEDs are also triggered by remote control, so the bomber can be hidden when the bomb goes off.

First developed by the Rhodesian army in the 1970s, MRAP vehicles are specially designed to withstand attacks from IEDs and land mines. The Pentagon deployed more than 26,000 MRAPs to Iraq and Afghanistan to protect troops from IEDs. MRAPs are characterized by their V-shaped hull, which deflects the explosive force of a land mine or IED underneath or near a vehicle. The force is pushed outward instead of up into the vehicle, protecting the crew inside. It is the latest enhancement to the design of four-wheel drive, light utility vehicles. It will eventually replace the standard vehicle of the army, the high-mobility multipurpose wheeled vehicle (HMMWV), or "Humvee," which has been used by the military since the 1970s. The Humvee answered many of the army's needs for a vehicle, but it is not perfect. Its main weakness is that its basic lightweight body is very vulnerable to attacks by IEDs.

The introduction of MRAPs to the battlefield has significantly reduced the number of deaths and injuries caused by IEDs; up to 40,000 lives have been saved, according to some estimates. The Pentagon has credited the design and technology of the MRAP with saving thousands of lives, and former secretary of defense Robert Gates has been quoted as saying that MRAPs are ten times as safe as Humvees in an explosive blast.

This MRAP (front) was constructed specifically for the rugged terrain of Afghanistan.

Mine-Resistant Ambush-Protected (MRAP) Vehicle

WEIGHT: 14–18 tons (13–16 metric tons)
LENGTH: 19 feet (6 m)
WIDTH: 9 feet (3 m)
HEIGHT: 9 feet (3 m)
CREW: 5–10 personnel
OPERATIONAL RANGE: 600 miles (966 km)
SPEED: 65 miles (105 km) per hour

US soldiers use an MRAP to block off the town square of a small village in Afghanistan.

Alternative Fuels Save Lives

All vehicles used in combat run on gasoline. That fuel has to be imported and delivered with trucks to very remote areas where the military is fighting. These convoys of delivery trucks are highly vulnerable to attacks by insurgents and IEDs. The less fuel that the Humvees, tanks, and MRAPs use, the less frequently these delivery trucks have to make these dangerous trips. So, the military is increasingly employing alternative fuels like solar power. One marine company that installed solar panels in the Helmand Province in Afghanistan reduced its fuel consumption by 90 percent.

CHAPTER 2

Humvee Beginnings

In 1979, the US Army wanted a new vehicle—something that was versatile and could replace several existing vehicles. The army jeep, the all-terrain cargo vehicle known as the "Mule," and the army ambulance had all been in use since World War II. But, having three different vehicles meant that soldiers who operated and took care of them had to learn about all three machines.

The army was ready for a vehicle that could serve as a combat machine equipped with weapons and also act as a combat-support vehicle, carrying troops, supplies, and medical equipment. It wanted a machine that could operate in a number of very different environments.

A vehicle that was safer and performed better was also desirable. Ideally, the new vehicle would be faster, lightweight, and better able to move cross-country quickly. This new vehicle had to be a "jeep on steroids." The Humvee was born.

The Humvee is one vehicle that can do many jobs. The work of lighter jeeps, heavier all-terrain cargo carriers, and army ambulances was all taken over by the more versatile Humvee in 1985. The Humvee was first used in combat in 1989 as part of Operation Just Cause, the US invasion of Panama.

Although Humvees are large, they are lighter than some of the vehicles they replaced. Humvees are also easier to take care of, are more reliable, and stand up better to heavy-duty use over time. Humvees are also very mobile. This means that they move easily over many different surfaces. Four-wheel drive helps Humvees operate everywhere from sandy deserts to rain-soaked jungles, and from steep mountains to bumpy, unpaved roads. They can even drive across the bottom of a five-foot-deep (1.5-meters) river without floating away.

Humvees can travel hundreds of miles, with only small amounts of maintenance. They must often carry their cargo and passengers safely while dodging bullets, bombs, and mines (explosives hidden in the ground).

Humvees are tough. Their bodies are made of aluminum, a metal that does not rust. The body and its special shock absorbers are designed to bend and give on bumpy, rutted, or rocky terrain, where other vehicles might crack or come apart. This gives the Humvee a longer life. Humvees also have special tires called "runflat" tires. Even if they are punctured, they allow the vehicle to keep moving. These tires have very thick walls that can support the tires even if they lose air pressure. The driver does not have to stop, get out, and fix or change the tire. This is especially important in combat situations.

In some Humvees, the tire pressure can be changed from the driver's seat to adapt to changing terrain. The Humvee now has power steering and is easier to drive than the old jeeps and trucks it replaced. A Humvee moves slowly and steadily over rough terrain. However, it can reach speeds of over 70 miles (113 km) per hour on paved roads. It also has high ground clearance, which means that its

FACT

Humvees in Panama

In 1989, deep in the Central American jungle of Panama, the US government had a place where thousands of gallons of fuel were stored in large tanks. This fuel was used to run US military vehicles in Panama. The United States feared that terrorists could attack the storage area, igniting and destroying the fuel. Secret sensors were hidden around the fuel tanks to detect movement. If intruders entered, a signal was sent to a group of four marines hiding out a short distance away in the back of a Humvee.

These marines and their Humvee were part of the US Marine Corps' special operations forces, known as reconnaissance, or "recon" marines. The Humvee's crew pretended to perform psychological operations, or PSYOPS, blasting rock music throughout the jungle to make the terrorists nervous. But this was just a cover for their real mission. They were really spies, watching for and identifying any trespassers without their presence being revealed. The detailed information these four hidden marines collected helped the United States plan the US-led invasion of Panama to overthrow and capture the Panamanian leader at the time, Manuel Noriega.

Night Vision

Humvees can carry many weapons and pieces of equipment. One of the most important is a night vision viewer. This allows soldiers on a Humvee to do surveillance, or spy, after dark. Night vision viewers and goggles work by collecting and boosting the tiny amounts of light that are still available at night.

The lens of the night vision viewer collects extremely tiny particles of moonlight or starlight. Then discs inside the viewer change and magnify the light particles to thousands of times their original size. The particles next strike a green phosphor screen, which glows brightly with the image of the night scene in the viewer.

body sits very high off the ground. This allows the Humvee to travel over rocky, snowy, or densely overgrown terrain.

A Variety of Uses

The Humvee's most important feature is its versatility, the ability to change and do many things. Its design allows it to be changed for many different uses. No matter what the Humvee is doing, though, its engine, chassis (body), and transmission (the system that moves the vehicle) stay the same. Many of its other parts can be changed depending on the Humvee's mission.

One use for a Humvee is to transport troops. For this purpose, extra benches are added in the cargo area. Humvees are also used to carry shipments of cargo, like food or medical supplies. Sometimes they carry shipments of weapons and ammunition. In this case, the cargo area is left open with no seats. At other times, the Humvee is fitted with powerful weapons of its own, like machine guns or antitank missile launchers. Then the Humvee becomes a combat vehicle.

With a special attachment called a winch, which mounts at the front of the Humvee frame, the Humvee can be used to tow other vehicles or to rescue vehicles that have gotten stuck or have flipped over. The winch's cable, motor, and hook can pull other vehicles out of ditches.

Finally, Humvees can be used as ambulances in combat zones. When set up as an ambulance, the Humvee can carry either four wounded soldiers on stretchers or eight wounded soldiers sitting on the built-in bench seats along each side of the rear compartment.

Humvees can transport people, cargo, and weapons. They can tow and rescue other vehicles. They can function as combat vehicles fitted with weapons or can help save lives as ambulances. Humvees are easy to operate and take care of. They can do all of these things in a variety of places, from open deserts to dense jungles and raging rivers.

A missile flies out of a launcher mounted atop a US Marine Corps Humvee.

What Goes on a Humvee?

Machine Gun

One of the main weapons that can be attached to a Humvee when it is being used as a combat vehicle is a machine gun. Machine guns can fire many bullets very quickly. A Humvee's machine gun is mounted on a turret. The turret allows the gun to rotate in a complete circle so that its operator can fire bullets in any direction.

Night Vision Viewer

This special piece of equipment is used for nighttime surveillance (spying) missions. With it, soldiers are able to see better in the dark.

Antitank Missile Launchers

These tubes are mounted on the roof of a Humvee. They are used to launch missiles, which are powerful explosive weapons that can destroy tanks or other large vehicles.

Winch

A winch is a machine used to tow vehicles or equipment or to pull them out of ditches. It includes a spool of thick cable with a hook on the end and a powerful motor, which rolls up the cable after it is attached to whatever vehicle it is trying to help.

Loudspeakers

Five-foot-wide (1.5 m) loudspeakers can be attached to the roof of a Humvee for blasting loud music or making announcements. These are used for psychological operations (PSYOPS).

The Proving Ground

Before using it in combat, the army tested the Humvee for more than 600,000 miles (965,606 km). Drivers took the new vehicle over rugged courses that imitated off-road conditions in combat environments around the world. Humvees were driven over rocky hills, through deep sand and mud, in water up to 5 feet (1.5 m) deep, in desert heat above 100 degrees Fahrenheit (37.7 degrees Celcius), and in arctic cold at temperatures of -20 degrees F (-29 degrees C).

A US Marine directs the driver of a Humvee across a river as they travel through Afghanistan's rugged terrain.

Simple Supply Carrier

Perched on the border of Serbia, in the former Eastern European republic of Macedonia, Army Private First Class (PFC) James Toole was facing bad weather and difficult terrain. In the driver's seat of his Humvee on a fourteen-hour drive, he had just finished climbing a narrow, winding, steep mountain road that was almost impassable when it began to rain. He drove on.

The rain grew heavier as the Humvee descended into a valley on the other side of the mountain. A wide river cut through the valley. As the rain continued to fall and the Humvee rolled slowly along the now muddy, slippery road, the river swelled, rising nearly to the edge of its banks. Despite the bad weather conditions, the mission had to be completed. It was not exactly a typically heroic mission by Hollywood's standards, but that did not make it any less important—or any less dangerous.

It was 1993, and PFC Toole was there as part of a United Nations Protection Force. US Army troops patrolled the dangerous border. Toole's mission was to bring much-needed food to these troops. He carried eggs, fruit, milk, and meat in a cooler. The supplies had to get through or the troops would be stranded with nothing to eat in an area filled with opposing soldiers.

Although Humvees have seen their share of military combat, the all-purpose vehicle often proves its worth as a simple supply carrier. This mission was no exception.

Joining Toole on this mission was Staff Sergeant Johnny Castillo. Castillo rode shotgun, tightly clutching his automatic weapon. Attacks by warring troops were common on these supply runs.

The Best Vehicle for the Mission

The Humvee was the best vehicle to deliver the supplies because it could handle the almost impassable mountain roads.

The Humvee approached the river. Then it continued—right into the swollen river. The Humvee filled with water to increase its weight and to keep it from floating.

The tires gripped the bottom of the raging river. Slowly, the water in the Humvee covered Toole's and Castillo's boots. It was wet and uncomfortable in the Humvee, but they had to get across the river.

Once they reached the other side, the water drained out of the Humvee, and it continued along the bumpy road. Toole and Castillo passed several farms. Rounding a bend, the soldiers found the road blocked. The road was not blocked by troops, but by a large herd of cattle!

The animals plodded down the road, herded by a farmer toward a grazing field. Toole slowed the Humvee to a crawl. He pulled as far to the right as he could without tipping the vehicle into a ditch that dropped sharply from the edge of the road.

The soldiers grew frustrated by the delay of close to an hour, but it was nothing they had not encountered before. Toole was careful not to injure the cattle or the farmer and careful to keep all the Humvee's wheels firmly on the road.

The road wound further into the countryside. The quiet was shattered by a frightening sound—the barking of wild dogs. Attacks by these canines were a constant threat in the hills of Macedonia.

Castillo spotted the pack first. About a dozen wild dogs came tearing down the hillside heading right for the Humvee, barking and snarling. Castillo aimed his automatic weapon into the air and fired a few rounds.

The blasts echoed in the mountains. The dogs slowed their run, startled by the loud sound. Castillo did not want to shoot the animals and would do so only if he felt that his life and Toole's life were in immediate danger.

A convoy of US Marine Humvees travels in Iraq. Wild dogs can be a threat to military personnel.

Several of the bolder dogs moved slowly toward the Humvee. It seemed that the noise alone was not going to stop them. Aiming carefully, Castillo pointed his weapon at the ground a few yards in front of the lead dog. Then he fired.

Bullets struck the ground, scattering dirt in all directions. That did it. The dogs turned and ran back up the hill.

Toole remarked that it had been a close call, and Castillo agreed.

The Humvee rolled on. As the two soldiers entered the last village before reaching their destination, they were mobbed by a crowd of curious children. The enormous Humvee fascinated the local children. They ran beside it, touching the doors and fenders. Again, Toole had to drive extremely carefully to avoid injuring any of the children. Crawling through town, they finally cleared the group and picked up speed.

At last, they spotted the first border outpost along the road where the US troops were anxiously waiting for the Humvee. Pulling into the outpost, Toole and Castillo had many helping hands unloading the fresh food for their fellow soldiers.

After several more stops along the border, the two soldiers headed back to their base. The return trip was uneventful, and this routine mission was completed successfully. Toole and Castillo were proud of the way their Humvee had done its job. The Humvee was truly the only vehicle that could have made it to the outpost and back again safely.

Sink or Swim?

Most vehicles float when they enter high water. Not Humvees! They are actually designed to sink so that their tires remain on the bottom of a riverbed with good traction. Water comes into the vehicle through openings in the floor, increasing its weight and causing it to sink.

A Humvee can go across deep rivers, as long as the driver's head is still above water! A Humvee's air intake and exhaust pipes are tall. They stick up above the top of the vehicle like snorkels. This allows the Humvee to drive through very deep water.

The Humvee's engine is also sealed so that the ignition (starter) and other electrical parts do not get wet.

Just Dropping In!

Sometimes Humvees are parachuted into places that are difficult to reach. The vehicle is strapped to a metal platform, which has large parachutes attached to it. The platform, with the Humvee attached, is then dropped from the back of a cargo plane.

Unlike paratroopers, who can jump from planes or helicopters many thousands of feet in the air, Humvees are dropped from just a few hundred feet above the ground—or closer! While a person can steer a parachute after he or she jumps, a parachuting Humvee cannot be steered. So the shorter the distance it has to fall, the more likely it is to land where it is needed.

Troops then parachute down beside the vehicle, arriving exactly where they need to be, ready to begin their mission.

Humvees parachute to the ground at Fort Bragg, North Carolina, during an airborne training exercise.

Convoy Protection

Bullets rained down all around Sergeant Leigh Ann Hester. Explosions tore up the road in front of her Humvee, which was escorting a convoy of trucks carrying supplies. She knew this mission would be dangerous, but she did not know that she would be thrust into what soldiers called the "kill zone," the center of intense combat.

Beside her in the shotgun seat was Staff Sergeant Timothy Nein. It was March 20, 2005, and Sergeants Hester and Nein were National Guard soldiers in the military police (MP) in Iraq, part of the 617th Military Police Company of Richmond, Kentucky. Sergeant Hester's Humvee trailed behind the supply convoy. She knew that in recent months attacks by Iraqi insurgents against US troops had increased. The insurgents are Iraqis opposed to the US military presence in Iraq.

She jammed down on the Humvee's accelerator and pulled the steering wheel hard to the right. The vehicle took off, gaining speed. Hugging the side of the road, Hester sped past the group of insurgents in the trenches who were firing on the supply trucks. As Hester drove, Staff Sergeant Nein fired his automatic weapon into the trenches.

The mission of the 617th was to travel with the convoy along the busy supply route outside Baghdad, Iraq's capital city. They were to keep a watchful eye out for attacks from the sides and rear of the convoy. Hester and the eight other members of her company, all in Humvees, were armed and ready. They each had the same mission: to protect the convoy and make sure that the much-needed supplies arrived safely. They hoped not to engage in actual combat. But that hope would soon be shattered.

Suddenly, just outside of Baghdad, this routine mission became anything but routine when about a dozen insurgents attacked the convoy. They had been hiding in trenches alongside the road. They fired automatic weapons from the trenches and tossed grenades, or small bombs, at the supply trucks to try and destroy them.

Quick Thinking, Swift Action

Gripping the wheel tightly, Hester moved her Humvee in between the convoy of trucks and the attackers. She hoped to cut off their easy escape route. If they tried to leave the trenches to get away, they would have to get past Sergeant Hester.

Then she and Sergeant Nein leaped from the Humvee and entered the trenches, their rifles blazing. In the trenches, Sergeant Hester killed three insurgents with her rifle. The attack on the convoy had been stopped.

When the battle was over, twenty-seven insurgents were dead, six were wounded, and one was captured. Three members of the 617th Military Police Company unit were wounded. But the convoy reached its destination safely thanks to the quick thinking and swift actions of Sergeant Hester.

The Afghan National Police, supported by the US Army,
travel in US Humvees on a mission to search houses
for unauthorized weapons in southeast Afghanistan.

Second-Generation Humvees

In 1995, a second generation of Humvees was introduced. This new model, called the A2, features a bigger and more powerful engine. The original Humvee had a 6.2-liter engine and could produce 150 horsepower (hp). The A2 has a 6.5-liter engine and generates 160 hp. The A2 also has an improved steering system and is slightly taller and longer than the original. The extra power and improved steering allow A2 drivers to move faster, more easily, and with greater control over rugged terrain.

A2 Humvee

Silver Star for a Woman

On June 16, 2005, Sergeant Leigh Ann Hester, vehicle (Humvee) commander, became the first woman since World War II to be awarded the Silver Star. The Silver Star is a medal awarded for gallantry in action, which means thinking of the safety of others before one's own safety. Hester received the medal at an awards ceremony at Camp Liberty in Iraq.

Sergeant Hester said that she was surprised when she heard that she was being considered for the Silver Star. "I'm honored to even be considered, much less awarded, the medal," she said.

Being the first woman since World War II to receive the medal is important to Hester. But she does not dwell on that fact. "It really doesn't have anything to do with being a female," she said. "It's about the duties I performed that day as a soldier."

Hester has been in the National Guard since April 2001. She said that she did not have time to be scared when the fighting started. She also did not realize the impact of what had happened until much later. "Your training kicks in and the soldier kicks in," she said. "It's your life or theirs. You've got a job to do—protecting yourself and your fellow comrades."

Sergeant Leigh Ann Hester

CHAPTER 5

Troop Transport

Traveling through the "Triangle of Death" always required some extra vigilance. Just south of Baghdad, this dangerous part of Iraq was known to be a lawless area crawling with insurgents who hid out in abandoned farmhouses and old munitions (weapons and ammunition) factories, just waiting to attack American and Iraqi troops. On this particular day in April 2005, Sergeant Joshua Haycox was carrying troops from the 3rd Armored Cavalry Regiment, and he knew they could be attacked without warning.

Looking for Insurgents and IEDs

Sergeant Haycox drove his Humvee slowly, keeping a safe distance from the Humvee in front of him. His vehicle was one of four armored Humvees traveling in a line. Their mission was to seek out and stop insurgents who had been attacking American troops and Iraqis in Baghdad. The Humvees had machine guns attached to their rooftop rotating turrets. The soldiers stationed behind the machine guns, called gunners, could fire them in any direction, spinning the weapons in a complete circle. The gunners were ready in case the convoy was attacked.

As Sergeant Haycox drove his Humvee, he scanned the road for roadside bombs. These IEDs had been exploding unexpectedly, damaging Humvees and killing or injuring soldiers all over Iraq. The Triangle of Death was one area where soldiers were likely to encounter IEDs.

The gunner in the turret of Haycox's Humvee stayed low, lifting his head out just far enough to see. Suddenly the Humvee just in front of them exploded. It swerved into a ditch and came to a sudden stop.

Haycox's commander, Colonel H.R. McMaster, ordered him to pull off the road immediately. The colonel was hoping to avoid any more bombs. He ordered the gunner to stand ready. Haycox watched as injured soldiers stumbled out of the bombed Humvee. Then, he realized that he had been riding in that same Humvee just ten minutes earlier. He could have easily been one of the injured. But there was no time to think about that. Gunfire broke out.

Haycox leaped from the Humvee, firing his rifle.

"Look for the triggerman!" shouted Haycox's gunner from up in the turret. "I can't find the shooter!"

Haycox kept his head down as he raced to help his injured buddies from the bombed Humvee. Colonel McMaster radioed for help. "We have encountered an IED and small arms fire," the colonel reported. "We need medical help and air support."

Soon two Bradley Fighting Vehicles carrying additional soldiers came roaring down the road. The huge, heavily armored tank-like vehicles stopped and dropped their rear hatches.

The soldiers on the Bradleys rushed out and crouched alongside a wall to direct their fire at a farmhouse near the bomb crater. That was where the shooting was coming from.

Bradley Fighting Vehicle

The Bradley Fighting Vehicle is a large tank-like vehicle. Its main role is to move troops, provide fire cover for soldiers during a battle, and defeat enemy tanks.

This heavily armored vehicle has several weapons. It has a chain gun, which can fire single shots or many bullets like a machine gun. The gun is powered by a motor that moves a chain through the weapon. As the chain moves, it loads and fires bullets, then ejects the used bullet cartridges all in one smooth motion. The Bradley also has an antitank missile launcher and two grenade launchers.

Bradley Fighting Vehicle

A US soldier looks out from the turret of a Humvee during a mission in Afghanistan.

Humvees as Ambulances

When the rear cargo area of a Humvee is set up to be used as an ambulance, it can carry up to eight wounded soldiers. It usually also carries medical equipment such as oxygen and intravenous supplies (for IVs), as well as a full supply of first aid equipment, including bandages, antiseptic, and splints. At first the ambulance Humvee was the only Humvee with air-conditioning. This was important in order to keep injured soldiers as comfortable and stable as possible. But now the newer up-armored Humvees all have air-conditioning.

During a field training exercise, soldiers get ready to move a simulated patient from a Humvee ambulance.

A cavalry scout searches for enemy movement while manning a gun mounted on a Humvee.

Within minutes they had captured five insurgents. Then two Apache helicopters swooped down firing automatic weapons. The remaining insurgents fled.

The helicopters landed, and medical workers, called medics, rushed to the damaged Humvee. Sergeant Haycox helped the medics treat the wounded. Then, he helped them load the injured into the helicopter. They were flown to a nearby hospital. Some of the injured survived, but others did not.

Sergeant Joshua Haycox knew he would never forget that day. He would also never forget the fact that it very easily could have been him injured or killed in the Humvee explosion.

So You Want to Drive a Humvee?

Humvees are versatile vehicles that can be used for many military operations. Soldiers who train to operate them must learn to drive and maintain them in all different types of terrain—off-road; over steep, bumpy dirt roads; and through rivers. They are also trained to drive into a battle area. They learn to maneuver when the Humvee is being used in combat (with a gunner on top) or to speed to the rescue while driving an ambulance-version Humvee.

When the training is complete, a special Humvee driver's license is issued to the soldier, who is then authorized to drive the vehicle. Training usually lasts between five days and two weeks.

All branches of the US armed forces use Humvees, but they are used mainly by the army and marines. Special training is required in order for a soldier to be approved to drive a Humvee.

The navy is not usually associated with operations on land, but Navy SEALs also use Humvees. SEALs are special operations troops highly trained in approaching targets on land from the air and the water. ("SEAL" stands for SEa, Air, and Land.) These highly skilled sailors must also be trained in driving Humvees for land-based attacks. They need to be able to move into areas quickly and get out undetected. If they are detected, they need to be able to outdrive their opponents in order to get away.

Humvee drivers practice driving cross-country in large convoys. In this case, drivers must learn to protect the convoy, while keeping all the vehicles together. This includes blocking intersections in city streets so that convoys can roll through safely.

To simulate combat situations, instructors shoot at student-driven Humvees with paintball guns. Sometimes instructors yell in the ears of students to shake them up, simulating the noise and chaos of a combat situation. Instructors will also fire weapons from inside the Humvee so that drivers can get used to the sound of returning fire being sent out by their fellow soldiers in the Humvee. These simulated combat situations help get soldiers ready for the difficult duty they will face when they drive Humvees in real combat situations.

Soldiers who drive Humvees while in the military are well prepared for many jobs outside the armed forces. This includes truck, bus, fire engine, or ambulance drivers. Their Humvee training and experience make them able to handle the special pressures that such drivers face every day. For example, those who choose to become ambulance drivers must often be able to drive their vehicles through busy city streets while still obeying traffic laws. They must balance the safety of other vehicles on the road and of pedestrians with the urgency of the medical condition of the patient they are carrying.

Since soldiers who drive Humvees have experience in high-pressure situations, some decide to become emergency medical service (EMS) technicians after they leave the military. These

A Humvee disembarks from a navy landing craft utility.

Training at Home

Lots of soldiers currently serving in Iraq drive Humvees. Many of them learned how to drive the large vehicles back home in the United States before they went overseas. There is a 550,000-acre (222,577-hectare) training facility in northwest Florida where soldiers learn to drive Humvees. Steep hills, deep rivers, and rugged roads simulate the environment soldiers will encounter once they are in the Middle East.

workers are often the first on the scene of an accident. They must determine the condition of any people hurt in the accident and do what is necessary to prepare them for their trip to the hospital. Then the EMS technician works with the ambulance driver to get the person to the nearest hospital as quickly as possible.

No matter what career a Humvee driver chooses after serving in the military, there is no doubt that the valuable training and experience gained behind the wheel of this multipurpose vehicle will help prepare the soldier for anything he or she decides to do.

A med staff sergeant drives a Humvee to transfer an injured soldier to the hospital.

A US Army sergeant adjusts a radio in a Humvee in Baghdad.

Disaster Training

Humvees are not only useful, versatile vehicles for combat situations. They also work well during disaster relief. Natural disasters such as hurricanes or tornadoes disrupt or destroy people's lives and homes. They can even destroy entire cities.

Those trained in driving Humvees can race to the rescue in these situations, confident in their vehicle's ability to drive through rough or damaged terrain. That is why the American Red Cross offers its volunteers training on Humvees.

US Marines drive a Humvee through the streets of Port-de-Paix, Haiti, working to provide medical, dental, veterinary and engineering assistance.

During a mission in Afghanistan near the Pakistan border, soldiers fire a Humvee-mounted grenade launcher toward suspected Taliban positions.

1941–1945—The army jeep called the "Mule" is introduced.

1985—The Humvee is introduced.

1989—The Humvee is first used in combat in Panama.

2007—The MRAP is introduced in Iraq and Afghanistan.

US military Humvees travel down Boylston Street in Boston on April 16, 2013. After two explosions occurred at the Boston Marathon, the area was a crime scene.

GLOSSARY

chassis—The body of a vehicle.

convoy—A group of vehicles traveling together.

grenade—A small explosive device that is thrown by hand or launched at its target.

gunner—A soldier who is stationed at the top of a Humvee and who operates the gun mounted on the turret.

improvised explosive device (IED)—Homemade bomb hidden in an everyday object that can be remotely detonated.

insurgent—Someone who opposes government, military, or political authority. Iraqi insurgents are opposed to the US military presence in Iraq.

mine—An explosive device usually buried in the ground.

mine-resistant ambush-protected (MRAP) vehicle—A vehicle, which will eventually replace the Humvee, designed specifically to better withstand IED attacks and ambushes.

missile—An explosive device that is fired at a target on the ground or in the air.

munitions—Weapons and ammunition.

night vision viewer—A device that allows people to see in the dark by collecting and boosting the small amounts of light that are available at night.

PSYOPS—"Psychological operations," used to keep the opposing side nervous and uneasy.

riding shotgun—Riding in the seat next to the driver.

runflat tires—Tires that can work even after they are punctured.

surveillance—Watching in secret; spying.

transmission—The part of a motor vehicle that sends power made by the engine to the wheels, enabling the vehicle to move.

turret—An armored revolving tower in which a gun and gunner can be stationed on a tank or Humvee.

FURTHER READING

BOOKS

Adams-Graf, John. *US MRAPs in Action.* Carrollton, Tex.: Squadron/ Signal Publications, 2013.

Dalet, David, and Christopher Le Bitoux. *The Jeep: History of a World War II Legend.* Atglen, Pa.: Schiffer Publishing, 2013.

Ware, Pat. *AM General Humvee Manual.* Somerset, England: Haynes Publishing, 2014.

WEB SITES

army.com

The US Army's recruiting Web site.

defense.gov/home/features/2007/mrap/

Department of Defense Web site on MRAPs.

globalsecurity.org/military/systems/ground/hmmwv.htm

Information about many types of Humvees, including ambulances and up-armored Humvees.

H1 Humvee

INDEX